The Pasty

Hettie Merrick

Tor Mark • Redruth

The Tor Mark series

Pasties in history

Cornwall, it is said, is the land of saints and pasties. This old saying is not as odd as it seems: Cornish people are fiercely defensive of their traditional food, and linking their favourite meal with the saints is a natural combination of spirit and body.

Perhaps because of the remoteness of Cornwall, joined to England by a mere thread on its northern coast and by Brunel's great iron bridge over the Tamar in the south, Cornish food has an identity of its own. Hearty and solid as befits a working community, it has some surprisingly expensive and unusual treats. Many visitors to the county never come across a 'proper' piece of heavy (hevva) cake; try clotted cream topped on a slice of syrup-spread bread (thunder and lightning) or taste real saffron cake, a rich curranty yeast loaf, golden and delicately flavoured with the most expensive spice known to man.

It might be more fitting if it were saffron cake which were linked with the saints. Every week of the year, somewhere in Cornwall, a village has a saint's day. Many still celebrate 'feast days' in fine style and it is usual to distribute huge saffron buns as a treat to all the children; but it is the pasty, plain, substantial, and made with the simplest of ingredients, that is nearest and dearest to every one's heart.

I hope this little book will explain the reason why.

First published 1995 by Tor Mark
PO Box 4, Redruth, Cornwall, TR16 5YX
This reprint 2002
© 1995 Tor Mark
ISBN 0-85025-347-0
The cover illustration is by Beryl Sanders
The wholemeal pasty recipe on page 31 is reproduced by kind permission
of A & C Black (Publishers) Limited
Printed in Great Britain by Cornwall Litho, Redruth

Pastry rolled out like a plate,
Piled with turmut, tates and mate,
Doubled up and baked like fate,
That's a Cornish pasty.

This old rhyme sums up the homeliness of the pasty, which is baked and eaten in most Cornish homes every week, and there can be no doubt that, properly seasoned and made, the pasty has a place among the great dishes of the world.

We know that it has been the mainstay of Cornish people for at least 200 years but its age and origin are obscure. I was very surprised to discover that a pasty was mentioned as early as 1300 ('All of pasties be the walls of flesh, of fish, and rich meat'), and that the cook in Chaucer's Canterbury Tales appears to have been a rogue who reheated his pasties and pies. In July 1537 one John Hussee sent to Queen Jane Seymour 'three pasties of the red deer, caused to be baked without lard. I trust this pasty reached (thee) in better condition than a pie of partridge sent before.' History assures us that the pasty did her no great harm even though, according to a researcher, she was in France at the time.

The English Dialect Dictionary (OUP, 1905) defined a pasty as 'a meat and potato or fruit turnover (Cornwall)'. It also stated that Cumberland, Yorkshire and Lancashire folk enjoyed 'a pie made without a dish, with the pastry rolled around the fruit or meat' and that children in Lincolnshire regularly took jam pasties to school for their dinners in the 1890s.

Eighteenth century accounts from up-country travellers to Cornwall tell of labourers bringing up their families on a diet of vegetables baked in a barley dough in the ashes of the fire. A West Briton report in 1867 tells of the subsistence level at which the miners lived and reveals their great dependence on flour. Many of these early writers expressed surprise that both children and adults looked reasonably well nourished on what they considered a very poor diet. Then, as now, the pasty had its detractors, but as a complete meal in itself it found a place in the hearts and stomachs of the Cornish who are proud to claim firmly that the pasty 'belong' to them.

The first pasty I cooked

My own fascination with pasties started early. I vividly remember the first time a pasty made an impression on my mind. I was staying with an aunt who lived at the bottom of a long lane in an isolated old farmhouse called 'Lower Content' and was standing in the kitchen by a scrubbed wooden table. It was pasty day and my aunt asked me if I would like to make my own.

I was ten years old and it all seemed so easy. Aunt Hettie shook flour from a large cotton bag into a bowl, chopped in some fat, poured in some water and soon there was a mound of pastry on the table. Turnip, onions and potatoes were soon prepared and the beef cut into chunks. She sliced salt off a loaf-shaped block and fetched the pepper pot. Like most children I was used to rolling out pastry for jam tarts so my round looked reasonable, but somehow I couldn't manipulate the potato and get nice even slices to fall onto my pastry. Aunt's left hand kept turning her vegetables easily while her right hand sliced at a furious rate. Before I got to crimping, I was in trouble. I could not get the pasty together. Aunt's mountain of filling was all safely gathered, the edges neatly turned over and her pasties waiting to go onto the sheath, which had a shower of flour.

It took me a time to patch up my holes, crimp, and put my initials on the corner, though there could be no doubt which was mine! The pasties were brushed with milk and put into the Cornish range, the fire having been 'caught' with twigs to get a good blaze to start them off. While they were cooking, the table was cleared and covered with an oilcloth, then with a white tablecloth for Uncle Fred's dinner.

Aunt and I took our pasties outside to eat, wrapped halfway up with paper We sat on a large blue slate which covered an engine to pump water. Nearby a stream trickled past, shadowed by a huge sycamore tree shedding aeroplane seeds down on us. The birds sang and hens clucked around the mowhay. It was the lovely summer of 1939 and high above the sun shone relentlessly in a blue sky. They were lovely pasties and this day remains as one of my happiest memories .

The double-ended pasty

There is a widespread view, particularly among our visitors, that a true Cornish pasty should have jam or apple in one end and meat and vegetables in the other. They are genuinely disappointed when their search for one is in vain. I have never met anyone who has made or eaten such a pasty, though I have seen two recipes, one in a little booklet compiled by members of St Gwinear Church, the other in *British Cookery* edited by Lizzie Boyd (see page 31). There may be others, but I have found no mention of such pasties in historical records.

The mass media may be responsible for the idea of a dinner-and-pudding pasty catching the attention of the public, as the idea seems to tickle the imagination of cookery writers, but most of us locally take it with a pinch of salt. Jam or fruit, meat and vegetables, cook in different timescales. Besides, eaten in the hand (the proper way to eat a pasty) the further corner gets ever tastier as the juices settle in the bottom end.

But, like all stories, there may be a grain of truth in the tale. My grandmother certainly always made sure that she had enough pastry left over from pasty making to roll out a large round of pastry for 'jam paste'. She would spread half the uncooked round with a little butter, fold it over and bake it unglazed. When cooked it was split open, spread with jam and then with cream she had scalded from the milk. This was our 'afters' – after the pasty.

Jam pastes may have a link with a savoury-sweet pasty – but would that original have been baked or boiled?

Someone kindly sent me the recipe of a Bedfordshire clanger, a suet roll containing meat and vegetables one end and jam the other, separated by a bridge of suet pastry. It was steamed for about two hours and taken out at dinner time to the men working in the fields. I can understand that this suet roll would cook successfully, but if it were baked, the bridge would not form a seal in the same way.

When my daughter was a child, she was taken to visit the parents of a cousin. There on the stove was a large pot puffing out steam. Being a curious little girl she asked what it was. Uncle

George told her he was boiling a pasty; he had a dry sense of humour and I suspected he must have been pulling her leg as I had never heard of anyone boiling a pasty, but on checking up I found that he sometimes made a large suet pasty which was tied into a white cloth and steamed in an enormous dark blue enamel pot used solely for this purpose or to boil the Christmas puddings. It was cut and divided into portions for all the family. My uncle worked as a shipwright at Falmouth dockyard and, as it was a long way to go each day, lodged in the town during the week; his land-lady, a Miss Maken, regularly boiled him a pasty. This was boiled in water, but I have been told by Mrs Truran of Camborne that she often makes small beef pasties and cooks them in a broth, which sounds tempting.

Broth was always on the go at my grandmother's house where it was bolstered up with lovely light dumplings which grew enor-mous as we watched them cook, covering all the liquid. Ours were plain, but Grandfather had currants in his and called it figgy duff. We ate some dumplings with our dinner and the rest for pudding with 'tracle' (syrup) poured over.

It is not so long ago that food was either roasted over an open fire or boiled in an iron pot resting on a brandis in the hearth. Families were brought up on a surprising amount of suety fare and before the 1939-45 war almost all pastry was made with suet or dripping. Often, even today, a roll of this pastry is placed around Cornish under-roast – a pan of meat and potatoes in water with a couple of whole onions and a little dripping or but-ter, baked in the oven. A few families still prefer suet pastry for their pasties, but the texture is a bit bumpy. Perhaps at one time a jam and savoury double pasty was boiled and enjoyed but, once oven-baking became possible, was tried and found wanting?

The Cornish range

Pasties as we know them probably came into their own with the Cornish range.

Cornwall was the cradle of engineering and Holman's of Camborne probably made the first domestic solid-fuel stove. There was a huge demand for this new invention, which replaced the cloam (earthenware) oven; soon foundries in towns all over

Cornwall were making ranges. Trinity House installed Cornish ranges in all their lighthouses, and even fishing boats were fitted with small versions. They cost a fortune, or so it seemed to ordinary folk, but everyone who could scraped together the £5 or £6 needed to buy one.

They were prized possessions, blackleaded till they shone and the brass knobs gleamed with frequent polishing. For the first time women had some control with their baking. Pasties cooked to perfection; once in the oven they stayed clean, browned nicely, and you could let the fire down and the pasty could simmer or 'soak' as we say. Many of us recall, with a sigh, the taste of pasties cooked in the 'slab', as the iron range was soon affectionately called.

Not everyone could afford an oven and in the early 1900s many people took whole dinners, trays of pasties or cakes to the local baker to be cooked after the day's bread was out of the way. This practice continued in Torpoint at least till very recently, where friends remember with amusement a neighbour throwing her sheath of pasties at the wall. They had come back from the baker black and ruined.

Coal-fired ranges were in common use all over the country till the 1950s, when they were gradually replaced by Raeburns and Agas using cleaner fuel, or by gas or electric cookers. A few people refused to get rid of their slabs, and they are still going strong, each with its own temperament as anyone who has ever owned one knows.

I am told that a 'combination micro-wave' will bake a pasty, but I am too set in my ways to believe that it will do so properly. Pasties need time to enhance their full flavour.

Miners and pasties

Miners have always had a special and strong association with the pasty and it is interesting that a hundred years ago pasties were being eaten in four particular counties (Lancashire, Yorkshire, Cumberland and Lincolnshire) all so far from Cornwall. Perhaps the Cornish miner took the pasty with him when he travelled to the northern mining areas in search of work. Certainly for men who worked in one of the most arduous occupations known, the sturdy pasty was a hot, tasty and cheap meal. It 'stood by ee' and Cornish miners took one to work every day. These men often had to walk miles to get from their homes to the mine and then descend by ladder into the bowels of the earth and sometimes walk far out under the sea before beginning their day's or night's work. Time made no difference, for all was darkness lit only by the single candle on the men's headgear.

Many mine owners provided large ovens at the surface specially to keep pasties hot for the men, and dinner time must have been a welcome diversion. Cornishmen are very fussy about their food and everyone would want their own. Pasties vary according to taste and pocket, so it was important to get the right one.

Many jokes and tales were told, especially against new wives who still had to improve their cooking. One tale is told of a young wife unwise enough to enquire whether her husband had enjoyed his pasty; she was told, 'A wadn' no good at all, time I got down to fifty fathoms a were scat to lembs [broken to bits]. The wans Mawther made wadn' break if they'd faaled to the bottom of the shaft.' She had made her pastry with too much goodness.

Around 1875 the price of tin plummeted and miners went abroad in droves to find work. Soon, it was said, you could find a 'Cousin Jack' (a Cornishman) at the bottom of any mine any-where in the world. As soon as they could, the men sent home for their sweethearts, wives ('Cousin Jennies') and families; but wives weren't much good without the pasty, and some sent home for the slab as well.

I wonder if any of those Cornish ranges are still in existence in faraway places – Mexico, South Africa, Canada, South America and Australia. In many of these countries the strongest legacy left by the miners may have been the pasty and it is comforting to know that there are pasty shops around the world wherever the men settled. As 'at home', the pasty is a must for most occasions.

When the Australian Cornish hold their gatherings, thousands of pasties are consumed in a few days and I have heard that there have been attempts to declare pasties the state food of Michigan, where the pasty outdoes the hamburger in popularity and is held in such regard that a whole day is devoted to its honour.

About a century ago there was a very resourceful woman who lived in the Camborne area. With her donkey and cart she drove around the village of Troon every day at 11 o'clock. Every few yards she blew a whistle and housewives brought out pasties, each in a named bag which she delivered about two miles away to the men and women working at Holman's Works and some of the mines nearby.

There was a lot of work at the surface where women ('bal maidens') were employed breaking up ore with long handled hammers, in noisy and demanding conditions for about £10 a year. At some places where ore was smelted, pasties were kept warm on cooling blocks of tin. Through all such treatment the pasties would stay intact, warm and safe in their edible containers.

Deep underground in a mine there are all kinds of sounds. Water drips and there are echoes of work in neighbouring workings. The miners sensed the presence of 'the little men'. Legend has it that the miners left the ends of their pasties for these 'Knockers' or 'Knackers' as they were called. This offering seems to be a paltry one, but the miners had little enough to give and it must have been considered enough to satisfy the mischievous imps who were renowned for taking offence if slighted, but could be helpful if placated.

The 'end' of a pasty should not be confused with a 'corner', which is about a third of a pasty deliberately saved to be eaten later or else, as manners and custom demand, reluctantly offered to someone who happened to arrive just as you were about to eat.

My brother and sister-in-law recently went on a sea cruise from Falmouth. Although the weather was truly atrocious, it didn't stop them enjoying the lovely meals but on returning they were dying for a pasty. My sister-in-law, Sylvia, made pasties the next day rather than waiting for her usual pasty day later in the week. As she was putting them on the table, a grandson arrived, having cycled from a nearby village. She asked him if he would like a corner of her pasty, which he politely declined. Sylvia made a pot of tea which, drunk with sugar, is considered an essential companion to the pasty. As a rule, no Cornish person takes sugar in tea due to Charles Wesley demanding a boycott of sugar when preaching against the slave trade, but an exception is always made for the pasty! Sylvia again offered to share her pasty, and again her grandson replied, 'No, thank you.' So she sat down and cut her pasty in half.

It is very difficult to enjoy a pasty with someone looking on. You feel a distinct sense of guilt. So Sylvia said, 'Are you sure, my 'ansum?' and this time he said 'Yes, please.' But by now the pasty was already cut in half, so it was half she had to give away. My brother, whose pasty was much bigger, silently decided to leave a corner of it for her; but he enjoyed it so much that the last mouthful had gone before he realised he had eaten his pasty 'from end to end'.

Sylvia, of course, would have preferred to have made an extra pasty. All Cornish women are adept at stretching the ingredients to make one more pasty, often baking an extra one for a widower, a poorly neighbour (you have to be very ill not to be able to eat a pasty) or an elderly person, and I'm sure that many of our new residents from 'up-long' have been welcomed with a surprise pasty. My father-in-law was stationed in Falmouth during the first world war and his wife and baby daughter came down from Birmingham to stay for a while. She was young and nervous, but her landlady, Mrs Behenna, included her in when she made the weekly pasty and she never forgot it.

Pasties at sea and at Twickenham

Fishermen, like miners, had strange beliefs. It is not difficult to be superstitious when your daily life is dangerous and old age uncertain. Whilst fishermen would eat pasties at home, they would no more take one to sea than they would mention rabbits or go fishing after meeting a clergyman while on their way to the boat. Cadgwith fishermen, however, found a way of overcoming the ill luck: if they found that someone had brought a pasty on board, they would remedy matters by breaking off the ends. Perhaps this is connected with the old saying that the Devil, hearing that there were saints in every nook and cranny in Cornwall and that the Cornish would put just about anything into a pasty, was afraid to cross the Tamar in case he was put in one himself. When I was small, I remember being told to crimp the corners of my pasty securely to make sure the Devil could not get in. I suppose the fishermen wanted to be sure that he could get out!

I once had a pasty shop in Porthleven, a fishing village. Most days, three young men would come in to buy pasties to take with them for their day's fishing. They were not Cornish and they seemed to get a large share of the snags often encountered with gear and catches. I didn't like to suggest to them that perhaps they should not take pasties on board as I thought it would sound silly in this day and age, but I wonder...

When I was newly married, I foolishly sent my husband Joe, a Midlander, off to work on a crabber with a pasty for his croust. They were having an unsuccessful day, with pot after pot being hauled in almost empty. When he produced his pasty, the other two members of the crew flung up their arms in horror and said, 'No wonder we're doing no good, we may as well go straight in.' He never took a pasty with him again of course.

Just last year, my daughter Ann was offered a ride out from Cadgwith in a small boat which was to follow a local gig race. She got on board and a little way out realised she had keys belonging to someone on shore. They tried to return but the engine spluttered and refused to restart. The local lifeboat was nearby and, as it was on its way back to base, she was told she could go in with them. Very soon, the engineer reported a fault with one of the switches. He was puzzled and asked Ann jokingly whether she had any pasties on board. She laughed and said no. She has a pasty shop at The Lizard and had forgotten that she did, in fact, have a pasty in her bag for someone in the cove. Later that night the engineer rang her husband, another crew member. 'I've tracked down the problem on the boat,' he said. 'Good,' replied my son-in-law, 'what was it?' 'The trouble was your Ann's - - - - pasties,' was the forceful reply.

Superstitions are often very local; pasties in boats don't worry the inhabitants of Fowey, further up the coast. Every year as part of their Feast celebrations an enormous pasty is displayed outside the pillars and steps of an old inn, 'The King of Prussia', and distributed free to anyone willing to queue up for a slice. Fowey does not have an oven large enough to bake this pasty, which is about six feet long, so it is baked at Polruan, the other side of the river.

Currently it is made and cooked by Mr Minall, who kindly made time in a busy morning to tell me that though he is not Cornish he inherited the task when he took over Polruan bakery. I think he enjoys making – and giving – this huge pasty, into which goes 20lb steak, 70lb potatoes and 20lb each of turnip and onion; it needs 30lb of pastry to enfold it. The pasty is carefully transferred by stretcher to a barge which is towed across the river by a small tug accompanied by much noise provided by the Fowey 'band' – a collection of weirdly dressed men banging drums and blowing whistles and trumpets, without a note of music between them.

This kind of raggle-taggle band was not uncommon in many Cornish villages a hundred years ago, usually starting off the May Day revels, but their unruly ways and drunkenness were curtailed by a mixture of force and religion. Echoes of this may be haunting a similar band formed in Falmouth not so long ago. Called the Falmouth Marine Band, the men have their own smart uniform of Cornish tartan kilt and white shirt, and are comparatively restrained as they march along; they are keen supporters of the Cornwall rugby side, to the dismay of some but the entertainment of many, and give a tremendous roll of the drums at matches home and away, and especially when the symbolic pasty is hoisted over the goal posts at important matches.

Getting the pasty over the bar is fairly easy on home ground but it takes a lot of ingenuity to evade the officials when Cornwall reaches a county cup final at Twickenham.

This ritual began in 1908 when Cornwall beat Durham in the final at Redruth. Lake's, a local pottery firm, made three ceramic pasties. One fell from the bar on the great day, one was given to the visitors, and one is at Truro Rugby Club.

Large pasties are often made locally for fêtes and fund-raising events. A two-foot pasty was sent to a soldier serving at the front during the first world war, but the Young Farmers claim the record for the largest pasty ever made: in July 1985 a pasty 32 feet 1 inch (9.78 metres) long was displayed. It had taken four hours to make and three hours to crimp, and was baked in a specially built oven.

Pasty rows

The Cornish are not really obsessed with their pasties, but it is a fact that pasties creep into all kinds of conversations. Arguments on crimping and contents can crop up at any time on local radio programmes, when certain announcers love to stir things up a bit, and pasties often make headlines in the press, national as well as local. Not so long ago there was a report of a man in court charged with attacking his wife with a frying pan and hitting her with a broom handle because his pasty was not all that it should have been. This was a serious incident, but pasty stories are usually fun. Everyone enjoyed the story of a young woman sacked for eating a pasty during her dinner break at her employer's business. She had bought it from a rival firm and, to add insult to injury, the other baker was an Irishman, who promptly offered her employment.

Many people were outraged when they heard that a non-Cornish person had been awarded first prize for 'the best Cornish pasty' at a competition organised up-country. It was not the nationality of the winner which caused the furore, but the fact that carrots and peas were judged a proper filling. On this point Cornish people are united, one and all: these two vegetables in particular do not 'belong' to a pasty.

I must explain that Cornish people never call a pasty a 'Cornish' pasty, and that pasty is pronounced with a long 'a', as in 'part'. 'A pasty' to us indicates the traditional filling of potato, onion and meat, and most often swede (which is referred to in Cornwall as turnip). Any other pasty would be known by its filling – a liver pasty, a pork pasty, and so on.

It is a fact that in some parts of Cornwall turnip is not considered part of a pasty filling, but perhaps they were not grown locally and so were unavailable. Turnip is so necessary to my idea of a pasty that I was amazed when my neighbour in Stithians, where I lived for a while, never put any in her pasties. But then she was just as surprised that I did.

Sometimes within the family some will and some won't like turnip and there's a well-known joke about a mother who put the initials 'TT' in the corner of all her pasties. At dinner time she doled them out as 'tis turmut' to some and 'tidn't turmut' to the others.

I am indebted to Mr G Ladell of London, a gentleman devoted to the history of Cornish food, and particularly of the pasty. Mr Ladell ferrets out all sorts of interesting facts, ancient and modern, and sends them to the Cornish Studies Department, Redruth Library, where there is a real treasure trove for pasty-lovers to delve into. In one of his letters, he writes of the introduction of the 'swede' into Britain. He says that the plant, also called rutabaga, came from the part of Sweden where the Lapps lived in the 1750s; it was taken to southern Sweden by Carl Lynne, a Swedish botanist. One ounce of seed was sent to Scotland in 1786/7, where it was grown. The swede was popular and in less than ten years had reached Cornwall (around 1795) so I feel that perhaps my neighbour's recipe in Stithians was an older version than mine.

A few years ago I went several times with my husband and sister-in-law to the ten day Celtic festival in Lorient, Brittany, to make pasties. We always took a couple of sacks of turnips with us, as it was difficult to obtain them there. On one occasion we ran out before back-up supplies arrived with Ted Gundry, the well-known local radio personality. I used carrot instead and put up a large notice begging everyone not to betray me in Cornwall, which seemed to appeal to the French sense of humour, producing a lot of broad smiles.

Fish pasties

With Cornwall almost entirely surrounded by water and fishing traditionally a major industry, it would seem natural that fish would be as popular a filling as meat and vegetables but there is no evidence that it is or ever was. Most people shudder at the thought. Old postcards sometimes show pictures of pasties containing mackerel or pilchards, but I suspect they were published 'for the visitors' or for fun.

If there is one vice Cornishmen are guilty of, it is that they are great players of practical jokes. They love to tease, and the pasty often comes in handy. What could be more droll than to present a pasty-lover with a pasty filled with fish innards, an old shoe or a

14

piece of wood? Fish seems to be the most popular choice, often offered to a best friend. After a lot of amusement, a real pasty is usually produced.

The only true survivor of fish with pastry may be the star-gazey pie of Mousehole. The tale is often told that many years ago the people of this little fishing port were in dire straits and near to starving. It was mid-winter and there had been a spell of poor (a local expression for very bad) weather when the boats had been unable to put to sea. At last one Tom Bawcock chanced the weather and took his boat out, returning with a catch of seven kinds of fish. This miracle is celebrated each year just before Christmas when a huge fish pie is made with the heads sticking out of the pastry. It is consumed at a local pub with much drinking and singing, and Tom Bawcock's name resounds around the tiny harbour. The late R Morton Nance, a respected scholar and writer, suggested that this legend may have evolved from an older feast traditionally held during the third week of December by fishermen generally, the different kinds of fish representing hopes of plentiful and varied catches in the year ahead.

Miners also held their festivals at this time of year. Certainly a great fuss was made of Christmas, with villages having their own particular carols and plays; though most of these are now lost, some villages have managed to hang on to a favourite carol and Padstow still possesses a complete set which is sung each year.

Pasties get a rest at Christmas, but it's not long before you hear someone exclaim, 'I could murder a pasty.'

International comparisons

Food has been packaged in tasty edible parcels for many centuries; with pastry or dough for covering, a little expensive meat or fish can be made into more substantial mouthfuls.

In Russia and Poland, left-over meat or fish and vegetables are enclosed in a yeast dough and deep fried. The *empanada* of Argentina contains, in addition to cooked meat, hard-boiled egg and sultanas. The Italians make *panzerotti*, a pizza-dough-based turnover of egg, bacon and three kinds of cheese, unusually flavoured with a good helping of chopped mint.

In Mexico you might buy a highly spiced pasty, copied from the

Cousin Jacks perhaps and peppered up for local taste.

America's mining areas have various pasties, some even with carrot, and I have heard of a pasty containing both pork and beef, flavoured with celery and garlic.

Britain itself has long been famous for its puddings and pies. Similar to the pasty is the 'Forfar Bridie' of Scotland, a turnover of finely sliced shoulder steak with some chopped suet and onion in pastry.

The Cornish pasty is unique in two ways. Firstly the filling is always raw and is baked at the same time as the pastry. Secondly it is a meal in itself, leaving very little room for anything else other than something light like jelly or junket and cream or, often, just a cup of tea. It really is an insult to see pasties advertised with chips and they are never eaten with two vegetables and gravy in a Cornish home.

What defines a proper pasty?

Discussions are endless on the 'right' way to make a pasty. Even men argue on its finer points and some enter the men's or open section of the pasty competition at local shows. It may be a reflection of happy childhood days that it is often Gran's pasty that is lovingly recalled, but sometimes a younger person is singled out as 'having a good hand with a pasty', or even the ultimate accolade, 'She makes some ansum pasty!' Opinions vary as to what makes a handsome pasty, but there are a few golden rules.

Meat must be cut and never minced, vegetables sliced and not cubed. Potatoes should be 'old' ones which 'go abroad' nicely instead of staying in whole pieces as early or new potatoes do; and it is important to make a firm elastic pastry which won't fall apart. Traditionally plain strong flour was used for the pastry, but since the introduction of baking powder in the twentieth century some people prefer self-raising, though personally I think that pastry made with this flour absorbs the juices. Many bakers oblige by making both shortcrust and flaky pasties and the customer has a choice.

When I was a child I would be sent to the butchers for 'pasty meat' and he would know that he should give me either chuck steak or skirt. Up-country butchers may not recognise the word 'skirt', so familiar to Cornish cooks and it is often difficult to pin-point this elusive part of the cow.

Almost next door to my favourite ice-cream shop in Newlyn is an excellent hog's pudding maker, Lenterns, who sell their own-reared Aberdeen Angus as meat in their shops. One of their butchers told me that skirt is the lining for some parts of the cow's diaphragm. He also suggested that the reason why it is almost impossible to obtain outside Cornwall is that there is little or no demand for it, so it usually joins other odds and ends and gets made into mince.

It may seem strange that neither fillet nor rump steak are suit-able in a pasty but expensive and tender cuts of beef somehow lack flavour and texture. You might be tempted to use minced beef but it makes an inferior pasty, although shin, trimmed of gristle and cut finely, is very good. Some people swear by box-heater, which is shoulder steak or blade, but the meat in your pasty is a matter of taste and, if you are a large family, what you can afford.

There has been quite a fuss in the past that some shop pasties lack a decent amount of meat. According to the Trade Descriptions Act 1967 a pasty should contain at least 12.5% meat. This guide was probably needed and is not all that generous, but a lot is expected of 'bought' pasties which can never please every-one; I think that the increasing popularity of 'shop pasties' must be a tribute to the bakers who try very hard to make a good fair-priced pasty.

Beef is the most expensive item in the pasty, but please remem-ber that a pasty is not a steak pie! I am sure that many families were brought up with pasties made with a piece of meat in each corner and another in the middle, and my husband sometimes complains that I have ruined his pasty by putting in too much beef. Some people insist that you should not salt the meat as it toughens it. I always mean to try this but remember too late; habit is so strong and the salt has been shook!

You may think that once the ingredients are decided, loading them in the pastry case is straightforward – but in what order do you layer the filling? Should it be onion (or shallot) first, turnip next, then potato, or vice versa? Do you put the meat in between? or on top? or 'all mixed up like a Redruth pasty'?

And where should the pasty be sealed? A minefield, this one, some affirming that you crimp along the side and others that you must crimp across the top. There are so many experts in Cornwall on the correct way to crimp that perhaps we should create a new -ology, crimpinology. Good crimpers are much sought after, as advertisements in local papers prove, and it is quite an art to produce a neat crimp instead of a thick bulky ridge.

Should you make a hole in the top, or would the pasty cook better left whole? An experienced pasty maker automatically gently stretches the pastry round the filling and may not bother to make a hole, but there is a very good reason for putting a small slit in the top of a pasty The pasty is in fact a 'pressure cooker' in its own right. Steam building up inside can cause the pastry to balloon up away from the filling and you must take care that you never bite into a pasty too soon after removing it from the oven. The outside may feel cool enough, but the inside stays hot for a long while. It is strange that the slit works so well, releasing some steam while allowing the pasty to cook, whilst accidental holes and breaks do not, so always mend any other holes with extra pastry. Pastry too far separated from the filling would cost you valuable points if you wished to 'show' your pasty, so making a slit is advisable.

Do you egg-wash or brush with milk or just water? These things should matter if you want to compete in village competitions but judges differ and you can see people looking very puzzled at the prize selections. None of my aunts brushed their pasties with anything other than water or milk, but my mother always whipped up an egg. This, combined with her buying such things as mushrooms and toilet rolls, caused her father-in-law, a retired fisherman, to say 'Ida's all right, but she's an extravagant woman.' He put this down to 'London ways' she had learnt when in service in the big city.

I think the only solution to all these problems is that the way you have been brought up to make your pasty is the right one.

Personalised pasties

Within a family there will be likes and dislikes. Mine take pasties as they come but some might request no onion, no turnip, a little or no pepper; others may want parsley, or kidney which was specially bought to put in the corners of father's.

This may be the reason why everyone's initials are put on the left (some would say right) hand side of a pasty with a spare length of pastry, but it is useful too if you want to save a corner to eat later. There can then be no argument about ownership at supper time. Initials or a mark are also useful if the pasty is taken away from home to be eaten at work. Anyone will warm up a workman's pasty, but there might be more than one. I can remember my husband fuming for a week after someone at work took his pasty by mistake. He often laughs, though, at the memory of a friend's face: in the morning he had given his pasty to their boss's mother who lived nearby. She was a dear old lady from up-country who kept them well supplied with tea. At dinner time when he went to fetch his hot pasty, she handed it to him, straight from the fridge!

It reminds me of a fisherman working on his boat in a local cove who took his pasty to be reheated at a nearby café. At dinner time he went to collect it and was told he could have anything to eat except the pasty. The owner of the café had not been able to resist the smell of it warming up and had eaten it. I don't know if she has been asked to look after another, but I do know that she has been presented with a 'fish' pasty. The same lady committed the cardinal sin of eating her husband's left-over corner. She got up to let the cat out at 4.30 a.m. and could not resist the morsel left on her husband's plate.

Pasty stories

My daughter Ann makes and sells pasties at the Lizard and she and her husband Tony seem to have difficulty escaping them. Last year they took a well deserved holiday on a small Greek island before the start of the season; the local shop had nothing in English except *She* magazine, which Tony bought. Settling himself under a shady tree, he opened the pages and startled Ann by

19

jumping up and exclaiming 'I can't get away from them any-where!'

There in front of their eyes was a full page picture of a pasty on a cliff with a backdrop of Rinsey minestack. What's more, it was actually one of Ann's own pasties, taken a few years before for another magazine at a time when she and I were in partnership in Porthleven.

Ann was once contacted by a member of a yacht's crew taking part in the Fastnet race who thought that pasties would be a good meal on board and had written to ask for a booklet I had published on Cornish food. Tony suggested that he could, weather permitting, sail out with a batch of pasties as this yacht rounded the Lizard. Unfortunately (or perhaps fortunately if superstition is to be believed) the race organisers of the Royal Ocean Sailing Club ruled that pasties could not be sent out from land, as that would be classed as 'outside assistance'.

Long before Ann had a pasty business she had introduced Tony, whose roots are in Sussex, to the weekly pasty. It was a gentle introduction and for some weeks he kept saying that he could have eaten a bit more, so one day she made a pasty as large as she could fit diagonally in the oven.

When he came home he took one look at it, grabbed the tray and cloth from her hands, and disappeared up the road. Tony sometimes called in at the pub for a drink on his way home from work and that evening he and his friends had been discussing pasties and boasting as usual that their pasties were so many inches over the sides of their dinner plates. He plonked his pasty on the bar in front of his friends to prove his claim, and amidst much laughter he was recognised as the outright winner.

Every family has its own anecdotes and I wouldn't be surprised if there's been a man in every family who delights in offering his false teeth as an aid to crimping. When I was a child I hated it when my uncle teased us in this way, but such jokes may have disguised an eagerness to show off the fact that a person had a new set of teeth; in those days many old folk were toothless and often too poor to afford replacements. Sadly, pasty eating could get difficult in old age.

Pasties are so much a part of the vocabulary of everyday life in Cornwall that you could be offered a pasty nut (Brazil nut) or a pasty of orange. No one needs to share an orange now, but my grandmother used to peel an enormous Jaffa and divide it up into pasties for each of us children. She used to save the peel to simmer gently with sugar till it candied, and carefully folded up for future use the large coloured square of tissue paper in which the orange had been wrapped. Nothing was wasted.

Oggies

A pasty is often called an 'oggy'. No one seems to know how or when this name originated, but it is particularly popular in Devonport and Plymouth where sailors call them 'tiddly oggies'. Tiddly in naval slang means proper, and as 'proper' is the most common word used by Cornish people, both as adjective and adverb, to describe anything (proper job, proper 'ansome) tiddly oggie – proper pasty – makes sense.

Some people suggest oggy comes from hoggan, a kind of bag the miners carried their croust in. Years ago, many miners ate vegetable pasties as they could not afford meat of any description, but some were fortunate enough to be able to keep a pig, or 'hog'. Dr A K Hamilton Jenkin, a noted authority on Cornish social history, referred to a miner's croust called hoggan, 'a lump of unleavened dough in which was sometimes embedded a morsel of green pork. This fare, although heavy enough to kill anyone who had not been inured to it since youth, long remained general among the miners.' So possibly oggies came from hoggans, and were pork pasties.

Cornish people on the whole dislike 'oggy' as a word for pasty, but as the youngsters like the word, I suppose we are stuck with it. Cornish rugby supporters have adopted the chant 'Oggie, oggie, oggie, oi, oi, oi,' when cheering on their team, and the cry is no longer confined to rugby. Football supporters use it, and even ladies have been heard 'oggying on' their Cornish team at a ladies bowls final.

The commercial pasty

The aroma of pasties is unmistakable and the smell of them in the street tempts many holiday-makers to try one. Most bakers' pasties are good, and millions are sold each summer; some connoisseurs spend a lot of their time on a pasty trail, looking for perfection. It is a good idea to watch out at mid-day for a baker's shop with a queue of local people spilling out of the doorway.

It is very difficult for me to pass comment on the packaged pasty. Making my own weekly pasty I have never tried one, not even in the interests of research, unlike Mr Ladell who religiously tries every new variety he finds on supermarket shelves, and donates the wrapper to Redruth Library to be recorded for posterity. Such pasties do provoke passionate reactions in letters to the press and complaints on radio, but it would be unfair to judge a warmed-up, mass-produced item against a hot freshly baked one.

A few years ago while walking round a local catering trade fair I was surprised to see a 'Cornish pasty mix' on sale. On investigation I was shocked to discover that it contained dried vegetables and meat that was to be reconstituted with water to put into pastry, and this, it was claimed, would make 'a Cornish pasty'! I was even more shocked that the young man selling the product spoke with a nice Cornish accent. He looked a bit contrite when I told him I was ashamed to see such a thing on sale in Cornwall, but he told me there was a certain market for pasty mix here. In no way can this be called a proper way to make a pasty and we should all be up in arms about it.

Perhaps this kind of filling decided Mr Martyn Hawkins of Martin's Bakery, St Austell, to suggest in 1993 that there should be a competition for the best 'trade' pasty in Cornwall. Alarm bells had rung the year before when the National Association of Master Bakers held a pie and pasty competition in Birmingham and the winner of the Cornish pasty class contained sweetcorn, peas and lamb. When Mr Hawkins became President of the Cornwall branch, he and his fellow members set about organising a local competition which was held at the Royal Cornwall Agricultural Show at Wadebridge. The competition promoted a lot of interest on Radio Cornwall when Ted Gundry said that 'the Cornish Master Bakers have now set a standard for the traditional Cornish pasty' and a positive side effect was that the National

Association agreed that in future competitions Cornish judges will judge the Cornish pasty class.

On the whole I think most manufacturers make a good effort, but home-made pasties are in a class of their own, and I hope that readers may be prepared to have a go. It is not true that only a Cornish person can make a decent pasty so if you don't succeed first time, try again. But don't cook all your ingredients beforehand!

The essence of a pasty is that everything is cooked together. You must allow time enough, as pasties are a bit of a fiddle to make, but think of the time you save on washing up! Beware though; your family may, like Cornish families, begin to demand them once a week and for every occasion from picnics to weddings and funerals.

Pasty pastry

One of the secrets of a successful pasty is the pastry and although shortcrust is often specified in recipes, this type of pastry is not popular or even liked by many Cornish cooks, who never rub in the ingredients to a 'breadcrumb' stage for pasties but instead roughly mix in chopped fats and flour with water, getting a more elastic dough.

Strong flour as used for bread making is best, but satisfactory results can be got from ordinary flour. If you must have a soft pastry, you could use a mixture of self-raising flour and plain. The amount of fat to flour is a matter of choice varying from half fat to flour, which is probably the most popular nowadays, to one fifth fat to flour (an old fashioned hard pastry). Many people use one third fat to flour.

Recipes usually say 'sufficient water to mix', which can be difficult to judge as you put more water in a pasty pastry than you would into shortcrust, so I have tried to be exact as to the amount, which can vary according to the flour and even the humidity.

It does help to have cold ingredients for pastry and sometimes I put the fats into the freezer for a little while and grate them into the flour. If you don't have a rolling pin, a wine bottle makes a good substitute in an emergency.

Pasty pastry, for four eight-inch pasties

450g 1lb strong white flour (large pinch salt optional)
100g 4oz margarine (Echo or similar hard variety)
110g 4oz lard
175ml 1/3 pt water

Put the flour and salt (if used) into a bowl. Cut off a quarter of the lard and rub into flour. Grate or slice the rest of the fats into the mixture and stir with a knife. Pour all the water in and stir until absorbed. Knead a little and leave at least 30 minutes in the fridge before using.

Pastry can be made the day before, wrapped in polythene and stored in the fridge overnight. Pastry freezes well, but remember to take it out the night before you need it. Do not refreeze.

Wholemeal pastry

This is preferred by some people, especially for vegetable pasties. Use vegetarian fats instead if you prefer.

225g 1/2 lb   wholemeal flour
225g 1/2 lb   strong white flour
100g 4oz   Echo margarine or butter
100g 4oz   lard or Cookeen
                salt optional
175ml 1/3 pt   water to mix

Roughly chop the fats into the flour. Rub in very lightly; pour in water and stir into a ball. Knead for half a minute and rest the pastry for at least half an hour.

Pasty filling, quantity for one pasty

50g 2oz   onion or shallot (some people like leek)
50-75g 2-3oz   turnip (swede)
100g 4oz   beef skirt or chuck steak
150g 6oz   sliced potatoes
                black pepper, salt

Making the pasties

Keep the sliced potatoes in a basin of cold water till needed. Trim any gristle off the meat and cut it (with some fat) into 6mm (1/4 in) pieces.

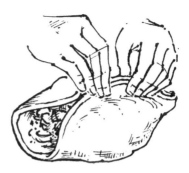

Place the filling in the middle of the round

Gather the two sides of pastry to each other and press firmly together

Generously flour the board or area you are using. This allows the pastry to relax as you roll, especially if you flip the pastry up from the surface every now and then. Cut off a quarter of the prepared pastry. Roll it out, keeping the shape, into a circle 21-23 cm (8-9 in) across. The pastry should now be the right thickness. Place an upturned plate over the pastry and trim round to get a good shape.

Place most of the turnip and onion across the centre of the round. Sprinkle lightly with salt and pepper to taste.

Place meat along the top and well into the ends; season the meat with a little salt. Top the meat with most of the potato and the remainder of the turnip.

Sprinkle again with a little salt, and add the remaining potato. Do not season the top layer: salt directly in contact with pastry can make it taste slightly bitter.

Dampen one side of the pastry with a little water. If you dampen the pastry all round or use too much water you will find the edges slide instead of sealing, so don't slosh it on.

Fold the damp side of the pastry to the other and press firmly but gently together, so that you have a seam down across the pastry, or by the side, whichever you find easier. From the right side if you are right-handed (or the left if you are left-handed) fold over the corner and crimp by folding the pastry seam over and over to the end. Tuck in the end well to seal. Alternatively, if you find this difficult, just curl the edge like a wave.

Crimping along the seal

Ready to bake. Note the slit in the top and the initials in the corner

Make a small slit in the top with a knife and patch any other breaks or holes with a little dampened rolled-out pastry.

Brush the pasties with milk or egg wash or even just water and place them on buttered paper or a greased and floured tray, leaving 5 cm (2 in) between them.

Bake in a hot oven 220°C (425°F, gas 7) for 20 to 30 minutes. Check the pasties. If brown, turn them down to 160°C (325°F, gas 3). Bake for another 20 minutes. Turn off the oven and leave them in the oven for another 15 minutes with the door shut.

Remove from the oven and with a slice lift the pasty onto a plate. Cut in half, allowing some of the steam to escape.

If you are eating them picnic style, place the pasties onto a cooling tray and wait 15 minutes before eating. If you want to eat them an hour or so later, or are taking them on a journey, wrap them straight from the oven in paper and then a clean cloth. Pasties keep extremely hot for a long time and if well wrapped a pasty made in Helston would still be 'hot' when you reached Exeter. I've even been told by holiday-makers that their pasties were still reasonably warm when they reached London.

Variations

Many people vary their pasties by substituting pork for beef, by putting in a mixture of kidney and beef, or by placing some parsley in one corner or sprinkled over the filling. Here, however, are some popular variations from what is usually thought of as the 'traditional' pasty.

Vegetable pasty

Use ordinary pasty pastry, or wholemeal pastry if preferred. Roll out pastry as for a pasty, then fill with layers of onion, turnip and potato, seasoning as you go, except the top layer. Seal, and cook as you would a pasty, reducing time by about 10 minutes. Just before dishing up, dribble in a good ounce of thin cream if you like it. Alternatively, while making the pasty put in about 25 g (1 oz) butter. With or without cream or butter, vegetable pasty is surprisingly delicious.

Cheese pasty

Use ordinary or vegetarian pastry. Roll out a 20 cm (8 in) round of pastry and slice onto it a small or medium onion and 50 g (2 oz) turnip. Season with pepper to taste.

Cover with 50-75 g (2-3 oz) grated or sliced Cheddar, or similar cheese. Add one medium to large potato along the top and season with salt. Place a few more slices of potato along the top. Seal and crimp. Cook as for a pasty, reducing the time by about 15 minutes.

Pork pasty

50 g 2 oz	pasty pastry
50-75 g 2-3 oz	chopped pork (with some fat)
25 g 1 oz	onion
	a few slices of cooking apple
	sugar, salt, pepper

Roll out pastry into an 18 cm (7 in) round. Slice the onion onto the pastry and add the chopped pork. Season lightly with salt and pepper. Cover with the apple and sprinkle a teaspoonful of sugar over. Fold over, seal and crimp. Bake for 20-30 minutes in a hot oven, reducing the heat when brown.

Beef pasty

Roll out pastry into an 18 cm (7 in) round. Cut enough meat, fairly finely, to cover one half of the round. Salt and pepper the meat. Add a layer of sliced onion, a sprinkle of parsley (optional) and a small piece of butter. Seal and crimp.

Egg or milk wash and bake in a hot oven for 20 minutes till brown. Turn the oven off and leave in the oven for a further 15 minutes.

Liver and onion pasty

To 200 g (7 oz) pastry add 25 g (1 oz) butter as follows. Roll out the pastry into an oblong; dot butter, at room temperature, over two thirds of the area. Fold uncovered pastry to the middle, and fold out the other third as for flaky pastry. Roll out. Fold in three again and leave for 30 minutes.

50 g	2 oz	prepared pastry
50 g	2 oz	sliced ox (or other) liver
50 g	2 oz	sliced onion

Roll out a round of pastry tea-plate size. Place half the onions on pastry. Cover with trimmed and sliced liver. Season with a good shake of pepper and salt. Cover with the remainder of the onion and seal as you would a pasty. Egg or milk wash and bake in a hot oven, 220°C (425°F, gas 7), for about half an hour, till brown. Reduce heat and bake for a further ten minutes. Eat hot or cold.

Egg and bacon pasty*

Roll out pastry the size of a tea plate. Trim rind off a couple of slices of streaky or any bacon. Cut the bacon in big pieces and place on one half of the pastry, leaving room for the egg in the middle. Break the egg carefully, leaving the yolk whole, and season it with salt and pepper. Dampen one edge and fold pastry over like a turnover. Use a fork to seal and make a pattern around edge. Egg or milk wash and bake in a hot oven for 20 minutes or so till brown on top and bottom.

Egg and sausage pasty*

Skin the sausage if necessary and roll it thinner. Roll out a tea-plate-size round of pastry, and dampen one half of the round.

Place the lengthened sausage in an oval shape on the damp side of the round. Break the egg carefully into the middle of the oval

---

* These pasties with egg are a little tricky to handle and this method may help. Pinch up the edges at the two corners, allowing a small portion left open, like a purse, then add the egg and finish pinching and fork the pattern on the edge. The Italian *panzerotti* are very similar to Cornish egg pasties; to prevent the egg escaping, breadcrumbs are included in the filling, which is all mixed in a bowl. This could be a method worth trying.

and season the egg. Leave whole, or break the yolk, as you prefer. Seal and fork a pattern on edge. Bake for 30 minutes in a hot oven, until brown top and bottom.

Egg and parsley pasty*

Roll out a round a little bigger than a saucer. Dampen one half. Sprinkle washed and roughly chopped parsley onto the undampened half. Add a little finely chopped leek if you like. Beat an egg, just enough to break it up, season, and pour onto the parsley. Quickly seal the edges of the pastry, taking care not to let any egg escape. Fork pattern on the edge. Bake for 30 minutes in a hot oven until brown.

Onion pasty

It is surprising how tasty tiny onion pasties can be and if you want a change from sausage rolls at a buffet you might like to try some. Use ordinary pasty pastry or, better still, pastry with butter added. Cut out 8 cm (3 in) rounds with a cutter or the top of a cup.

Put a good teaspoonful of finely chopped seasoned onion or shallot onto each round. Dampen one edge and seal; crimp or fork pattern.

Egg wash and leave for a few minutes. Egg wash again for a good shiny finish. Bake in a hot oven for 15 minutes or until brown. Turn off oven and leave them in for another 5 minutes or so. You could test one to see if it is cooked. A little cheese added is also very good; too much would seep through.

Buffet pasty

450g	1lb	made pastry
150g	6oz	meat, very finely cut
2 or 3		large potatoes
1		medium onion
		turnip to taste

Grate or finely chop all the vegetables. (Grating is not recommended for 'real' pasties as it would make them mushy, but it is all right for tiny ones.) Season carefully with salt and pepper. Mix the meat and vegetables together. Roll out the pastry and cut into 10 cm (4 in) rounds. Place a good tablespoonful of mixture onto each round. It may not be necessary to dampen the edges as the mixture is quite moist. Either crimp daintily or fork pattern around. Egg or milk wash. Bake in a hot oven for 30 minutes. Check, and if brown turn the oven down and leave for a further 10 minutes. The quantity should make 15 pasties.

Fish pasty

There is a recipe for a fish pasty in *Cornish Recipes* (published in the Tor Mark series but originally printed for the Women's Institute in 1929), but I don't think I shall ever make one.

Squab pasty

Take an equal amount of left-over boiled potatoes and turnip and mash well together with a good portion of butter or margarine. Cool if hot. Adjust the seasoning and place a couple of tablespoons of this mixture onto a saucer-size round of pastry. Place a piece of butter on top, seal and crimp. Egg or milk wash and bake in a hot oven for about 15 minutes.

Squab pasty (Mrs Lane, Carminowe Farm, Gunwalloe)

Roll out pastry and cut into tea-plate size. Place on it sliced cooking apple, a few sultanas, sugar to taste, a little spice and a nut of butter. Dampen one edge, fold over, seal and crimp. Bake for 15-20 minutes in a hot oven.

Date pasty

Use the pastry described for liver pasty (page 28). Roll out the size you require. Put dates into a basin and pour on boiling water. Drain immediately. Flatten the dates and place on one half of the round, to the edge. Fold over the other half and roll lightly with the pin. Score a couple of lines on top and egg or milk wash. Bake in a hot oven, 220°C (425°F, gas 7) till lightly browned top and bottom. Wonderful eaten just warm with clotted cream.

Jam or mincemeat pasties

Roll out saucer-size rounds and moisten the edge of one half. Place a tablespoon of jam or mincemeat in the middle and fold over the other half. Seal and mark with a fork. Egg or milk wash, and bake in an oven till brown. Always be careful that these pasties are cool inside before eating, and use a slice to remove them from the baking tray.

Windy pasty

'Jam paste', sometimes called a windy pasty, is made with any spare pasty pastry. They are popular with children, easier and less sticky for them to make than jam tarts or pasties, and there is no hot jam to contend with.

Roll out pastry to the size of round you require. Lightly spread butter on one half and fold over the other. Do not put a hole in the top; do not egg or milk wash. Bake in a hot oven for 15-20 minutes till cooked top and bottom. You will find the pastry rises, which may be why it is called 'windy'. When cooked, the pasty is split apart and both halves are spread with jam. Like date pasties, it is very popular eaten just warm, with cream.

Fruit pasties

Some people make fruit pasties, usually with blackberries and apple, but you have to be a very clever or lucky crimper to prevent blackberry juice seeping out.

'Whole-meal pasty' or 'Great pasty'

This recipe comes from *British Cookery* by Lizzie Boyd, a compendium of traditional recipes from across the whole island. I have personally not found anything like it actually in use in Cornwall, but it is an interesting recipe and from the time and temperature given it seems that the meat and vegetable filling may be pre-cooked. It is also amusing that the pudding end is as large as the savoury, but Cornish people are fond of 'afters', so it's not too surprising.

$1^1/_2$ lb shortcrust pastry $1^1/_2$ lb sweet filling
1 egg $1^1/_2$ lb meat and vegetable filling

Cut a small piece from the pastry and set aside. Roll the remainder out thinly and cut into 8 large rounds. Roll the small piece into a $2^1/_2$ cm (1 inch) wide strip and place across the large rounds to divide them into two equal halves.

Place the sweet filling in one half and the meat and vegetable filling in the other. Close the pasties towards the centre line and crimp the edges. Mark the sweet filling with an 'S' and the meat filling with an 'M'. Brush with beaten egg and bake for 30 minutes at 190°C (375°F, gas 5).

Conclusion

You can of course put 'anything' into a pasty. Most Cornish housewives make different pasties from time to time, but for the weekly pasty the traditional one is expected. Local cookery books do, however, give family recipes which have been handed down, and I have seen:

'Broccoli' (that is, cauliflower), par-boiled
'Herby', with shallots or onion, spinach, egg and bacon
'Leeky', with leeks, bacon and sorrel (sour-sops)
'Rice', stodgy cold rice pudding with a raw egg stirred in.

I believe I have seen a recipe for mackerel and date pasty, and chicken or rabbit are sometimes substituted for beef; but oddly, lamb or mutton is scarcely ever considered. This is surprising as sheep were raised in Cornwall on a large scale at one time, and grazed on the cliffs.

I once judged a vegetable pasty competition, and the selection and ingenuity of contents were remarkable. Between fruit and vegetables, nuts, rice and curried pasties, it was difficult to judge and I regret that I didn't ask for all the recipes.

There has always been a great deal of interest in the pasty. It has survived the criticism of 'nutrition experts' over the years and will, I think, withstand the threat of annihilation by microwave. Love or hate them, you cannot live in the county and ignore them; they are part of our way of life, a religion if you like, and a main theme of our contemporary folk lore. Here the pasty reigns supreme. Hamburgers, pizzas, curries and even fish and chips trail well behind, and long may they do so.

> For a hearty man's dinner 'tis ample fare,
> With naught too little nor none to spare;
> And here again it deserveth praise
> That when it has vanished its virtue stays:
> For it gives sweet ease to the scullery quean,
> Who hath nor platters nor knives to clean.
> So I wish him joy whoever he be
> That first found out the Cornish Pastie.